IT'S NOT EASY BEING A MOTH

It's Not Easy Being a Moth

by
Mark Lee Webb

Accents Publishing • Lexington, Kentucky • 2021

Copyright © 2021 by Mark Lee Webb
All rights reserved

Printed in the United States of America

Accents Publishing
Editor: Katerina Stoykova-Klemer
Cover Image: Odilon Redon, *Saint John (The Blue Tunic)*, 1892

Library of Congress Control Number: 2021939836
ISBN: 978-1-936628-73-5
First Edition

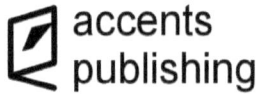

Accents Publishing is an independent press for brilliant voices. For a catalog of current and upcoming titles, please visit us on the Web at

www.accents-publishing.com

CONTENTS

I.

Mall Cool

Mall Cool / 1
In Miss V's English We Read Macbeth / 2
Creatures of Calabasas / 3
Transformation / 4
Jim Morrison Has Died / 6
Alice Cooper Is on *Midnight Special* / 7
I'm Out of Arm Reaching for You / 8
To My Guppy Who Does Not Trust Me Enough to Pick Her Up / 9
When You Learn All the Tricks / 10
To My Lab Partner Killed on a Motorcycle / 11
Spanish Class Field Trip to Olvera Street / 12
How Odd to Die Twice / 14

II.

It's Not Easy Being a Moth

It's Not Easy Being a Moth / 19
Big Insignificant Things / 20
Used to Be You Could Tell Which House / 21
My Wife Clings to Me / 22
Mosquitos / 23
A Better Kind of Science / 24
Parsimony / 25
Word Salad / 26
No, Wait / 27
If You're From Any Place But Here: *Warning Shot* and *Bullet Hole* / 28
What Happens When You Don't Wear Gloves / 29
I Don't Have Any Better Place to Be / 30
My Clubfoot Went to the Movies / 31
Postcard From Morro Bay / 32
I Don't Think I'll Be Here Much Longer / 33

I Carry a Gaff / 34
What to Do With the Bones / 35
After You Drove / 36

III.

It's the Vague That'll Kill You

It's the Vague That'll Kill You / 39

Acknowledgments / 61

About the Author / 63

For Molly

*Dedicated to My Parents
Jeanie and Lee*

I.
Mall Cool

MALL COOL

We circle inside Clyde Wallich
Music City listening booths munching
Morrow's Nuts between tokes

        my lips
        they are grape

while Topanga Plaza angels arabesque
behind Plexiglass   candlestick spirals
between Broadway and May
Company   Orange Julius with extra egg
glycerin drips down nylon fountain tubes
diffusing stoner brains

        my liver has goose bumps
        and that's the organ that stays warmest
        the longest after you're dead

    where did Billy Fletcher get this shit

it's ninety-five degrees in Woodland Hills
they're turning off the fountain
for the night
I better get straight

IN MISS V'S ENGLISH WE READ MACBETH

> *Being unprepared, Our will became the servant*
> *to defect; Which else should free have wrought*

while after class we take turns staring at a dildo
Everett Haskins found in Miss V's Camaro.
Wood. Metal. Everett's a stoner he takes all
vocations. Found the thing while her car was
in auto shop and he was adjusting the driver's side
bucket seat. Everett keeps it hid in the boy's head
where he hangs out between classes smoking
Chesterfield Kings. We pay him quarters to see it—

extruded semi-pliable plastic, factory-beige
flesh. Looks more like a bull walrus tusk to us
than a guy's bone. We're high school freshman
unprepared for *penises*. We never use the word
instead it's dicks and cocks, wieners, third legs.
We stand close to urinals in case a guy might
peek, unsure of normal, how big your Johnson
should be if you don't have older brothers.
Never this close to a woman before.

CREATURES OF CALABASAS

When your best friend tells you
his brother was treed last week

by a wild animal half-dog half-bear,
summer paints your canvas in shades

of rattlesnake and giant alligator lizard.
Your mom says be careful, tarantulas

are out seeking water, migrating towards
backyard pools. You wade only knee-deep

into surf at Zuma Beach, hoping lifeguards
at Station Number Seven take their eyes off

the girls from Encino long enough to spot
pods of killer whales migrating down

the California Coast that Mr. Myers
talked about in Oceanography class.

You stop hiking along fire breaks looking
for Indian relics and trilobites, afraid swirling

Santa Ana's might catch you on the wrong
side. That dude they say was murdered

by queers in the grape arbor, his body dumped
in a culvert next to the roadside rest area,

walks through morning fog rolling in waves
down Malibu Canyon. August in Calabasas,

school starts in two weeks, and you
know you'll be safe then because that

dude, the one always taking your
lunch money, isn't coming back.

TRANSFORMATION

It's hard to explain these teenage years,
or Uri Geller's spoons.
After Mott the Hoople
carried the news to all us young dudes
I started breaking out in spots—
stars falling from my face.
Mott was right you get tired,
concrete all around your feet,
your head, racing cats to bed.
You start to wear collared shirts
and listen to Elton John
on the easy FM side-of-the-dial,
trying to wait the weather out
but it's always the same in June
when your hills crinkle to ginger.
I should hop an empty box car,
try life as a gypsy moth shuffling
light to light until I find some patch
of dirt where two roads cross
with a single row of mud-straw shacks
that leak during rainy season.
Take up abstract art,
spend nights at a dive with a name
like Red's Tide, (a bar without a beach)
sitting in a booth by the door
where customers might sometimes toss
a few extra coins my way asking
for their portraits made.
On scratch paper I sketch them—
creatures with scaly snouts and lidless
eyes, my patrons reaching back into
the tip jar for refunds after I'm done.
The owner (his name is Red)
asks me to paint a mural along

the back wall where I stipple
sharks feasting on headless horses
swimming. But before I can finish
Red is nettled by a fever.
I try to help, drape amulets
of colored glass around his neck,
but the fever is too much.
Red's dead before morning's light.

JIM MORRISON HAS DIED

I'm eating pancakes at Sambos
thinking I'm so wasted
from Billy's party last night
maybe I'll thumb out to the beach
take a nap on the sand
don't even need a towel
when suddenly my waitress
tells me *Jim Morrison has died!*
and she goes on about how
sometimes he'd come in here
late at night for pancakes
before nodding off in a booth
did I know about
that one time in the Mojave
Jim saw dead Navajos
scattered all over the highway
one of the Indian souls
crawled right into his body
it creeped Jim out
so much he wrote *Peace Frog*
and I think well yeah
it's too bad about Jim
maybe today I'll thumb
out to the beach
climb over the jetty
crash Paradise Cove
and watch topless girls
on the other side

ALICE COOPER IS ON MIDNIGHT SPECIAL

tonight   I am sitting on my couch with Maria
she's humming *I Love The Dead*
while we wait for Alice and his guillotine
and when Maria starts to sing
Welcome To My Nightmare
I tell her she could be a star
another Janis maybe
and Maria says yes
Janis *full tilt boogie girl with smudge-pot voice*
and she goes on about how
her Papa bought a Janis album
after a week in Sebastopol
picking apples
but last year during strawberry season
in Carpinteria someone stole their hi-fi
maybe they'll get a new one
depends on how much cotton lint
they pick when they get
to Bakersfield next week

but tonight   Maria is sitting on my couch
waiting for Alice and his guillotine
it's only eleven
Alice hasn't come on yet
and Maria hums   she sings

I'M OUT OF ARM REACHING FOR YOU

Our walks to the 7-Eleven for a Slurpee now improbable
as the LA River, natural oil seeps in Summerland,
or creeks that are always dry but never the same twice.
Remember that science club trip to the coroner's office
where I exited through the gift shop? I know wearing
a stingray on your head is all the rage, their electrogenic
properties a cure for headaches, but I miss hunting
for blue-belly lizards with you (never afraid of grabbing
for their tails under rocks). In old Polaroids we ski Squaw
Valley slopes. Play volleyball in the summer at Zuma Beach.
We haven't listened to The Doors since your father
(ever the surgeon) handed you amputated arms and legs,
preparing his daughter for Drivers Ed. He stopped you
from going places where sand might stick to your feet.
Now you tell me ultraviolet blush looks better in the movies,
that I'm just another sunburn. But that won't keep me
from coming over every day and ringing your doorbell.
If you answer I'll undress you, wipe all the Coppertone away.

TO MY GUPPY
WHO DOES NOT TRUST ME
ENOUGH TO PICK HER UP

Just before I reach my hand into your bowl
you say *I'll bite*. Or worse, *I'll jump*.

I wish my fingers were kelp and you Angelfish—
not plain grey, not like the kind they sell
in pet stores next to live-bearing platies and mollies,
but an honest-to-goodness Anacapa Angel
fish swimming off The Point where you can hide
in my kelp-fingers during the day. Or at night
how often I don't stop breathing long enough,
hold my breath long enough, float to you as long
as you tell me how near to sharks we can dive.

WHEN YOU LEARN ALL THE TRICKS

girls say *You are cool*. I thought I could live on thimbles full of sparrow breath until Carolyn Shaw saw my scar at the beach and said it was gnarly. I started hanging out with a magician named Earl with fifty-two deuces in his deck. He gave me a dime, told me to go inside his tent. I saw Myrtle Corbin's four legs and Percilla the Monkey Lady. When a new girl transferred to our school and said she could levitate me, I told her *Sure, let's try.*

TO MY LAB PARTNER
KILLED ON A MOTORCYCLE

Our principal announced what happened this morning
and by the time Ronnie told your story in PE, you never
had mono in May, or a cold New Year's Eve. You left me
alone with our cat in Biology class, picked from a pile
of plastic-wrapped corpses before dissections started.
Remember how you stroked her head, still dripping
with formaldehyde, then demanded a scalpel, making decisive
cuts while other girls cowered? You told me never to believe
anything I can't hear. Like snow. Warned me about Lake Tahoe,
how it's too deep to freeze. Tonight, instead of going to your
funeral, I walked along Encino Reservoir, hoping for hail
because hail makes lots of noise.

SPANISH CLASS FIELD TRIP TO OLVERA STREET

    I walk alone
among the plaza vendors,
past a girl who wears a Dead Head tee,
who piles her hair to one side.
She stretches her body, hangs parrot
piñatas from a wire.

    Down an alley
there are boys in feather caps walking birds.
One of the boys says his canaria can tell my fortune
in Mayan for fifty cents, but Aztec
will cost a dollar more. I pay for Mayan
and the bird starts pulling threads
attached to a fortune
card the boy claims is all about the new car
I might perhaps with luck soon get.

    A sign inside El Mercado building—
        consiga el suyo temprano,
        a las once de su cráneo
        será elegido limpia
I write in my notebook and translate—
        get yours early,
        by eleven your skull
        will be picked clean
which doesn't sound right,
next to steaming goat head
with horns. And bags of grasshoppers
roasted with garlic and lime.

    I pick something more familiar to me
at a taquería called *El Pequeño Toro*—
crunchy corn tortillas filled
with carne, salsa, and queso—
then take my tacos

and a can of Pepsi Cola
to a bench, sit with my friend Steve
who's wearing his Día de Muertos
souvenir mask.

    After finishing, we catch up with a few
other guys from our school,
check out the main square.
Vendors selling flowers from carts
make it sizzle-cool,
while women holding bits of colored cords
dance in three-quarters time. A man tells
us they dance the *Baile de las Cintas*
and the song is a jarana,
how the women dance
around poles carved from branches
of sacred ceiba trees
that come from the Yucatan
where his mother wore chrysanthemums.
I guess not like the sad mums my mother kills
each fall when she forgets water,
how they smell like dirt and wood.

    When the dancing is done
and the flowers are all gone
we head back to our bus,
past the plaza
and the girl hanging parrots.
She sees me, flips her
unbraided hair to the other side.

HOW ODD TO DIE TWICE

listening to coyotes wager with the stars
on this first night of spring. Today at noon

my body casts no shadow for exactly two minutes
and now at night my shadow again disappears.

This is what it must feel like tripping on acid,
or tasting harvester ants washed down

with decoctions of jimson weed and white sage.
Not all of us survive. Some slip into the skull

of a swordfish adorned with dominos,
spend their time gazing at pictographs.

Others end up in Hollywood wearing Stetsons—
you can tell by how they sear their steaks

(Porterhouse, well-done). If you're from Encino
you might try on rouge and feathers, but friends

will still call you Vern. Over in Canoga Park
it's Groucho glasses, moustaches, and all that.

So many masks. The first time it happened to me
was last May when we ditched school for body

surfing. The water was cold, currents running down
from Alaska. I got hypothermia, turned purple,

felt sleepy. I couldn't stop shaking until revived
by dry blankets and Karen lying with me

pressing her body against mine. After which we
roasted hot dogs over a fire built from driftwood

washed ashore by storms some months before.
One piece was bent, a few rusty nails,

we all thought it looked like part of the bow
of some boat. I should have taken Karen

to the Junior Prom. I know she really liked me
and she's book-smart, wanting to go to UCLA

but Catie Shaw was into The Dead and wore
a violet bangle in her left ear. Catie gave head.

After school let out last summer Catie changed
her name to Starr-Fish and no one saw her since

someone said she hitched her way to Monterey.
This year I'll ask Karen to the Senior Prom,

borrow Dad's new Opel with ribbed corduroy seats.
It's only March, time enough for Karen to buy a dress.

II.

It's Not Easy Being a Moth

IT'S NOT EASY BEING A MOTH

Almost-butterfly. Spanish Moon. Chinese Luna.
Tiny scales diffracting light. Rub the wings

and illusion dissolves into fingertips.
You are here on a whim, a woman hued

because you slipped saying *I love you* first, landing
a season early. No one pays attention in the beginning—

threads from fibers of maguey plant,
the excessive number of sewing needles.

I wear the cotón instead of shirts, loincloth instead
of pants. Feet bare, no shoes. At night we sleep

in patterns of checkered embroidered pearls
you stitched from sultepeque cotton.

And this bruise I got trying on new hats?
I'm still waiting to see how we emerge.

BIG INSIGNIFICANT THINGS

Today my wife and I are rescuing stranded mollusks at Leo Carrillo Beach. She tells me not to toss them back—better to swim out beyond the break with a basketful and place each one on its own rock. I can't handle deep water, I really need a sea-blue wet suit. That's the safest color, because sharks are color blind. Ocean waves play every hue and none of them were written by Barry Manilow. She tries to soothe me *honey, to sing a suitable corridor, just once, we must morph into seaweed.*

USED TO BE YOU COULD TELL WHICH HOUSE

by the flowers.
Here, not much lasts long.

Before buying a bushel of moths
(Yellow Crown, Yellow Dream)

I warn my wife to sweep strays
out of our attic, that ripe avocados

give slightly when gently squeezed.
If it wasn't for the weather

we'd have missed each other.
On days it doesn't rain

we reseed dunes with native
plants. Sagebrush and salt grass

primrose and poppies.
Let stand barrel cactus

and coastal prickly pear, eradicate
invasive Mexican feathers.

Next month—strawberry pickers
in Camarillo. And the old bracero

squatting on the Safeway side lot.
To get here, take the fork in the road.

MY WIFE CLINGS TO ME

while sharks discuss whether they should drown her before separating us, some saying they did not know me without my clothes on. Just then a dolphin and two companion swordfish arrive carrying a sign of truce. Sharks at first do not believe, knocking one swordfish down. The dolphin intervenes, tells the sharks they will make peace on favorable terms. It is only then discovered that all trouble is due to misrepresentations of Barry Manilow. The sharks remain peaceably with the dolphins and swordfish, my wife and I recover our clothes, and we never hear what was done with Barry except he's not allowed in the deep end.

MOSQUITOS

It's the scent of carbon dioxide on my blue-tint lips attracting them. No longer lurking until dark, they bite me while I wait in Safeway's deli line for thinly sliced lacy Swiss. My wife noticed it first, when I cancelled our weekend trip to Hearst Castle after reading too many topographic maps. She tries to help, buys all my shirts. None gray. Or white, or beige. Says she's starting to feel like Juana Maria, who lived alone on San Nicolas Island surrounded by blue dolphins. Juana Maria, who sang the Toki Toki song *I live content because I can see the day when I get out* before her teeth wore down to pulps and gums. When my wife snuggles up to me (coy nymph) I slide away from her. What with all those swarms waiting for me on the other side.

A BETTER KIND OF SCIENCE

Whenever I suddenly start thinking about shadows when the sun simmers down to nothing how they disappear and the corners of our house lose their shape—my wife calms me. Says I need to wear less beige. I'm learning about colors from her. How prisms might explain dispersion, but they should be avoided. And shadows. How they're nothing-things, mostly irrelevant at night. And light. Years of waking each day at exactly six-fifteen a.m. to go to my insurance company job on the tenth floor of a downtown office tower and sit for eight hours at Desk Thirty-Five. Better, my wife says, to diffract, to follow the sun, how it carries a torch of tightly rolled bark to light the world. That after each daily journey across the sky the sun snaps the flame, throws sparks which are the stars.

PARSIMONY

On San Nicolas Island, indigenous men used cactus thorns
to carve the universe on their wives until the women bled,
then applied mezcal to produce blue tattoos etched
from eyebrow to breast. Women who wore shell beads

the colors of beginning-dawn sky. It is much later now,
I am married, and my wife tells me she never
had a lover who said *you are fine* which makes me feel
guilty for all the Rorschach tests answered *I just see ink*.

Forgive me. And all the other husbands who wear
hip waders, go surf fishing at Leo Carrillo State Beach
to avoid long conversations. Husbands who keep secrets—

    where to collect the best perch baits
of mussel and ghost shrimp.

    Channel Islands are out there somewhere
you just can't see them for the fog.

    Power plant smokestacks at Morro Bay never find
their way into picture postcards.

    The human body sheds six hundred thousand skin
cells every day but you never lose sight of a tattoo—

scars too deep to be erased by a woman's own flesh.

WORD SALAD

It is our anniversary. We aperitif
at one of those white-tablecloths

with waits dressed all in India
ink. I am wearing my oxford

broadcloth unbuttoned, royal blazer,
sand slacks, and a dinky around

my neck strung with one-half
of a snapper biscuit found

at the beach today. You
in strapless sequins, wearing

a dinky too, yours a bit more
elaborate with three common

jingles and two kitten's paws.
I am certain our wait is at this very

moment discussing us with the bussers
and slingers. Mocking our shoelaces.

If only they could hear us whispering
alligator lizard umbrellas   fence in the sombreros, quick

after the sand sprouts up
           we will be new enough.

NO, WAIT

I am smiling. You never can tell.
It's my incisors, worn to nubs
from biting my nails. You want

to save my teeth, offer chocolate
chip cookies to eat and ethers
to breathe. I take the cookies

but refuse to respire. After all,
I never listen for the noise a teapot
does not make. You try to levitate

me with curry from Bangladesh
and West Bengal spicy sea scallops
served with fresh-caught red snapper.

I still prefer salt and boiled potatoes.
I am sponge cake—cut me any way
you want, every slice is the same.

Remember when we first met
how one potted plant was enough?
Now you want more. You suggest

a shopping trip to Solvang, fill the house
with tulips and daffodils. But that's not me.
You forget the ranunculus I left rotting

in the shed, and the bromeliad lingering
on the back porch, its leaves curling—
an old man's gnarled toes.

IF YOU'RE FROM ANY PLACE BUT HERE: WARNING SHOT *AND* BULLET HOLE

I'm in a pallor, so my wife sends me to the market for tangerines. She knows I never learned to wait the weather out until it wrinkles June and our hills crinkle to ginger. Like Brooklyn Dodgers moving to Chavez Ravine which is part of Elysian Park. And Dennis Hopper came from nowhere, which is Kansas, which is why he now lives on Venice Beach and shot two bullets at Mao Zedong. The first one missed, sailing over Mao's right shoulder. The second got him in the eye. Exit wound—cilantro, or perhaps chayote squash. People do that sort of thing in California. Our climate is temperate.

WHAT HAPPENS WHEN YOU DON'T WEAR GLOVES

Trimming oleander along the back fence
might be easier than a few too many pills.
They'd say *he forgot to wear gloves*. Whatever
happens after that is none of my business.
Let my wife handle the details:
sparklers maybe. Taquitos fried just right.
Hire a juggler—the man from Venice Beach
with a hand hanging from his elbow.
Invite vatos in Eldorados selling pulque
liquor brewed in milk bottles. Thursday:
a classified ad for the antique shaving stand
I stored in the shed. She always liked the back
left leg, how it wobbled. And the lacquer finish
(not original). It's worth two-fifty but she'll
take seventy-five. That's why I married her.

I DON'T HAVE ANY BETTER PLACE TO BE

since you started staring at me like I was
a Pre-Columbian pot. In the middle I settled—
whatever road I drive now it's private access.
There's a food stand with the best chili cheese
dogs in Carpinteria, next to a Japanese nursery
selling Bonsai but their trees are brown and brittle,
need new pots, water, maybe a light root trim.
The owner pours warm beer into Hakusan flat tea bowls,
sets them along the walkway to catch slugs and snails.
This is where I go when I want to come home.

MY CLUBFOOT WENT TO THE MOVIES

in Westwood without you tonight.
Calloused, twisted at the ankle—

abnormality of connective tissues
knotted like a knobbly gooseneck gourd.

The movie was in a strange language
that only clubfoots understand,

with clubfoots wandering around
the countryside looking for their lost

families after some apocalyptic war,
asking *what happens if we go and find*

there is no God? In the final scene all
the clubfoots are standing in cow shit

inside a barn and they're all crying until one
of the clubfoots points to the top of the barn

where there is a stained glass window shining
psychedelic light on the cow shit and suddenly

the clubfoots start to smile and sing and dance
because the psychedelic light makes them feel

better about standing in cow shit all day.
After the movie my clubfoot limped home,

took a bath in copper sulfate and scraped off
mold between his toes. Slapped on a glaze

of glossy lacquer, then polished and buffed
until he transformed into a sort of gourd

birdhouse. Climbed on top our roof, hoping
for a rare pair of nesting purple martins.

POSTCARD FROM MORRO BAY

In a box of things you left behind—
sea urchin, slug, snail (extremes of low life)
I found a postcard addressed to me
without a stamp. On the front
is a picture of a man on a surfboard
holding an umbrella in his left hand.
Which is odd because the easiest way to keep
from getting wet is to avoid the ocean.
You can make someone believe
anything with a postcard. *Having a good time
wish you were here* that time you sent one from
Morro Bay. You tried to coax me *let's go
cliff diving*, you said *let's jump off Morro Rock*.
An inveterate matter to you, the distance
between sea and sky. You knew I was afraid
of heights, but still you teased me,
suggesting a trip even farther up the coast
to San Simeon, maybe Big Sur.
I could never go that high.
So I stayed home, alone, at sea level
digging holes in the sand. Burying myself.
Along came a tide and I disappeared.

I DON'T THINK I'LL BE HERE MUCH LONGER

It's the wrong exit, and I'm lost on my way
to Malibu Beach. I might not hear the freeway
if the car windows were up, but it's hot,
they're rolled down, and damn the adobe dust
dulling the view. I follow a detour down to dirt
on a plot of land marked only with tire tracks—

I don't think anyone really lives here. It seems more
like a spot to crash between seasons of dates and figs,
pieced together with sheets and scavenged boards.
I wave to a girl who's sitting on a floor made entirely
of discarded wood doors, a girl with coyote thistles
stuck to her socks. She tells me there's no place here
to swim. She says there's no beach. Just creeks
that always run dry but never the same way twice.

I CARRY A GAFF

in my left hand while I dive under
breakers hoping to spear a great white
(careful how you handle fish with no skin)
in Mexico, Ensenada or someplace like that
where very old men with their feet stuck
to the sand wade in lagoons
casting nets for crabs and sardines
and the next day a typhoon sweeps
all the old men out to sea
but I am still diving under breakers
and the next day too
after the typhoon
I am still in the water
diving under breakers
because on the beach there are broken shells
with sharp edges that will cut your feet
after the typhoon
I am still in the water
diving under breakers

WHAT TO DO WITH THE BONES

In Madagascar just before the monsoons
families dig up then buff the bones, dress

them in fresh silk lambas, raffia hats. I don't want
you spiffing me up before they weigh my heart.

Better to go alone like that bachelor cousin
twice removed who retired from the post office

at seventy, moved down to Orange County,
stopped showing up at our July 4th picnics

in Griffith Park. There is something graceful
about the idea of simply walking away,

drifting to a place where nobody knows me.
Take a studio by the week in Santa Monica

just a few blocks from the beach. Slip out
at night unnoticed, spend my last few

dollars at some dive bar where a beer
and a shot is still the drink of choice

before heading back to lie in bed
with my favorite Florsheims on.

AFTER YOU DROVE

from Ojai to the foot of Adobe Hill,
found the Chumash Kohsho near a grove

of sycamores, you came home and said
everything I told you was a lie.

You believe in sympathetic magic—
rattle carved of coyote bone to cure

crowning teeth. Hawk feather halos
stitched from fiber of milkweed

adorned with glass beads. Keep a cache
of polished charmstones for casting spells.

But California summers, all the hills crinkling
to ginger. Little ponds on little ranches

bake dry. Santa Ana gusts dust chaparral to
shades of buff-brown, the air sick with sage,

brush and scrub rolling down the arroyos.
I worry. Over sidewalk stains from walnut

shrubs in our front yard, August brushfires
scorching the shake roof, sea cliffs eroding

along the Palisades. You pick a mackerel's eye
from the claw of a crab and make-believe

it's a pearl. Swim with speckled sea snakes
in Morro Bay. Lay low, conjure me down.

III.

It's the Vague That'll Kill You

IT'S THE VAGUE THAT'LL KILL YOU

1.

On Olvera Street there is a canaria de la fortuna
and if you pay one dollar and fifty cents
the yellow bird will hop over to a box
and pick a paper slip
with your fortune
but the fortune is written in Mayan
or maybe Aztec   some sort of characters
not Spanish
not English
and only the brujo
who takes your money knows
I don't even think the canary can read it.

2.

Bottlebeetles do it right, adults living
on nectar while larvae consume the dead.
At eighteen I proclaimed *I'll never be
in a place where Big Sur is too far*
     my legs were short, I was still biting
my toenails. Now I limp
one block   to the intersection
of Winnetka and Ventura to buy fried
taquitos from the Mexican food stand,
passing by a discount store where late-shift
viejas behind the counter sell nitrous oxide
balloon hits to kids who live around the corner.

3.

Me and LA. It's complicated.
Like we lay together
in the same bed
but don't sleep
with each other.
Because this place is really
chicken noodle,
occasional stir-fry.
Cleveland in culottes.
Des Moines wearing Tommy Bahama.
Accidental fruit fermentation
    a layered acrylic interpretation of acid rain.

4.

I made it last night with a musty
Angelita   both of us stinking drunk
holed up in a Pasadena dump.
She said my hair wasn't
all that gray. In San Pedro
Humble Oil made four islands,
named them Grissom, White,
Chaffee, and Freeman. Decorated
pump jacks with pretties—
palm tree, waterfall, necklace of boulders
quarried from Catalina. Every dead astronaut
green-washed in nighttime Disney lights.

5.

Sometimes I stop
say hello   chat with young Angelitas
working the massage parlor next door
who blow promises through rings
of sandalwood incense burning
behind beaded curtains. I collect their bones
on Día de Muertos   decorate calacas
sugar-cube skulls with flowers—
Yellow Marigold   Gladiola
Yellow Marigold   every girl a petal.
Leave tissue-paper pillows
so they can rest after the journey.

6.

The dead don't lie   won't say
what bald spot?
I spend nights cruising Sepulveda
looking for Las Calaveras
sexy skeletons   elegant skulls
with powdered-sugar smiles
all heads and busts
barro negros sculpted black clay
skin slightly moistened
rubbed with curved quartz stones—
polished pieces I pull
from piles of matte grey.

7.

They lost Ah Fong and We Chung
when the Gold Line cut through east LA.
Workers wear respirators
sweep unclaimed cremains   agitate the air
with disinterred dust
    alluvial fans of powdered bone.

Chinese character for fan—
feathers living under one roof.
I name them
Zhang Mian   hiding face
Luo Shan   round face
every plume a person.

8.

California is out of water. All the palms are dead
but it's raining in Romania
where a man cuts graveyard grass
with scissors   eats a cheese sandwich   after that
he cuts more grass. I picnic with Orange County carney dwarfs
and immigrant Bucharest acrobats
in Evergreen Cemetery on the east side
of LA   have my picture taken
next to the cement lion   listen to aged midgets brag about that time
in '35 Sister Aimee Semple McPherson preached to the circus
about her resurrection in Agua Prieta—
    how Sister laid hands on the snake lady and cured scales.

9.

Dee Dee Ramone is buried in Hollywood Forever
alongside Valentino and De Mille.
Sunset Strip is shattered   all that's left are bags
of sugar skulls   and paper marigold
petals   every corner a Catrina or Coco working.
When they built the last freeway   scraped away
what was left of old LA
I tried living in Corona Del Mar
where there is an honest-to-goodness sunset
but breakers are swirls of asphalt
with *No Swimming* signs. I hate it.
Someone has to.

10.

I want to go for a swim
but there are sharks
on Sunset Beach.
I drive up the coast,
stay the weekend in Morro Bay
where a power plant
is cropped from the postcard.
Listen: sea lions barking all night.
I can see Morro Rock from my hotel
but there's a chain-link fence.
The guy who rents electric boats tells me
so rare birds can hide.

11.

It is Fourth of July and I am celebrating
by myself on Huntington Beach pier.
Sirens of scarlet lip and quivering thigh
skate by—teenage twins wearing identical white hot
pants and star-spangled halter tops   paper parasols
shelter skin from firecracker sun.

    Hamburgers from Ruby's Diner have too many onions.

Single surfer alone on south side
    I think   *I could never do that anymore*   safer to stay
on the crowded north shore   paddle out
just beyond the break   sit on my board
and pretend.

12.

Warhol said Paul Newman drinks Coke Liz Taylor drinks
Coke a Coke is a Coke and no amount of money can buy

a better Coke than the Coke the bum on the corner
is drinking. But Warhol was New York snow, he didn't

know we have more flavors here: snorkeler scouting
for sea urchins in waters off San Miguel eaten by a shark.

Diver hunting Anacapa lobsters drowns from the bends.
Girl with nineteen recent fillings in her notably bucked teeth,

multiple stab wounds and a slit throat found wearing
hip-hugging bellbottoms someone painted blue daisies

with red centers on, her body dragged across dust and scrub
and brush, dumped down an embankment off Highway One.

13.

There is a Cold War missile silo above Encino with the best
views. You can hike to the top and discover bomb bunkers

and surplus radioactive air filters. The city even installed
a water fountain. The last time up there a dog bit me.

The owner yelled   *If you're scared of big dogs you shouldn't be here.*
I said   *I'm fine with big dogs* and then he said   *you should go*

to the other side because this area is for big dogs. Since then
I have asked six other people if this side is for walking

big dogs. They didn't know anything about that,
but suggested I try trails by the LA River near

Elysian Valley and Frogtown. No one walks dogs
there, what with all the storm drains and gang tags.

14.

Flea market marlin nailed over my front door.
For luck. Dirty plates and a few longneck

Coors half-drunk sit on the table next to my
bed. It is ninety-five degrees in The Valley.

Because bones are dusty and dry this time
of year, relatives stack altars with slices

of watermelon and rice wine. Cover the face
of their thirsty ghosts with tissues smudged

with silver. I take a long drag on a Camel
then exhale real slow-like, roll over in my bed,

gaze out the window. How far is the ocean?
I always liked the ocean.

15.

Pieces of avocado did not smoosh in the salad spinner.
I'm all in. Bought a Powerball it is a billion dollars

because a tortilla fell to the floor. That clique
of clucked frubes from the beach—

the ones always making fun of me because
I'm afraid of being caught inside eating a heavy,

afraid of falling in the soup—
those same dudes came over to the house

and said anytime I want to borrow some board wax
just ask. Quick I fill my jean pockets with lucky lentils,

jump in my Gremlin and take the 405, betting only Valley-
bound lanes will be blocked at Sunset near Sepulveda Pass.

16.

Perhaps I won't go
to the beach   after all
that cloud
the one always over Catalina
that never moves
    maybe it will wake up
this morning all disoriented
and drift to Reseda.
        I'll drive over and watch it rain
        open my mouth
and catch big drops on my tongue—
think old-world chameleon.

17.

Zuma Beach under an umbrella
because it is misting
and wet   La Niña Mojada—
this is what you
expect in March.
I am reading a book
about a Chinese girl
her name is Huang Xiang
who fans the mat
on her parent's bed
cooling it down
so they might better sleep.

18.

Los Angeles is an orange, a cross between pomelo
and mandarin   Woodland Hills a divined graft
because navels don't produce seeds. It hasn't always been
like this. I was once an Aztec
ripping your heart out
while it was still beating
and you'd stare at it a long time
before passing out.
Now I'm on Pacific Coast Time
     three hours past due
planning to visit the Getty—
they say the goats are back, hard-nibbling fire breaks.

19.

These days I tell fortunes   read futures
cleaning lint traps (those doors of perception)
while I work second shift at *La Lavendería*
    white cotton   jogger's sock
    yellowed cotton   stoner's tee
every now and then conjure cash-for-smokes
      three quarters and a dime
      from an eight-year-old's
      lost lunch money.
My magic is three chords and the truth—
think Dee Dee Ramone
(can't play bass and sing at the same time).

20.

I woke up today thinking

I'll go to the beach / got there early fog never let up Catalina nowhere to be seen / I called it a day around noon at low tide / drove to Vons Supermart / collected carts in their parking lot / for every hundred you get a Century Chicken / tomorrow instead of trying the beach / I'll forget to wind the clocks / take my chicken / picnic in the park along Encino Reservoir / hope a storm maybe / starts something new like hail / because hail makes lots of noise

21.

I no longer dress in pelican feathers,
or leathers sewn with sinews of seal.
Afraid of condors, of live oaks
(how they cling to their leaves in winter).
December in Malibu and all the stars
are celebrating the solstice in Cabo,
this restaurant empty except for me.
I don't want to split for Baja
(those beaches have rocks all the same).
I'm tired, think I'll take the freeway home
    crawl into my caul
before I drown.

22.

I never planned on creeks
that always run dry but never
the same way twice. Never learned
to wait the weather out until
it wrinkles June and the hills
crinkle to ginger. A little of this
or a little of that missing each day.
Jimmy Page said your best days
are all about dynamics. Whisper
to the thunder invites you in.
Light and shade. You find mystery
in a shadow. But my best days?

They're scattered all over a mountain
near Malibu named Ladyface,
now a distant and gray impression
more glaze than granite.
There's a fog rolling around
these arroyos, smearing Ladyface
across my eyes. Are eyes
of a rattlesnake oblong
and peaked, or round?
I can't tell anymore—
there are too many shadows.
It's the vague that'll kill you.

ACKNOWLEDGMENTS

Several poems, or earlier versions, in this book have appeared in the following journals: *Aeolian Harp, Chiron Review, Clockhouse, Columbia Journal, JuxtaProse, Literary Accents, Louisville Review, Ninth Letter, Rattle, Reed, RipRap, Slippery Elm, Soundings,* and *Star *82.*

I thank Melissa Bashor, TJ Beitelman, Cathy Bowers, Gisele Firmino, Kari Gunter-Seymour, Bob Hicok, Michael Jackman, Marcus Jackson, Fred Leebron, Rebecca Lindenberg, Jon Pineda, Robert Polito, Buffa Short, Jeffrey Skinner, Katerina Stoykova-Klemer, my cohorts at Queens University of Charlotte, and the poets of the Columbus Salon for their support that made the writing of many of these poems possible.

ABOUT THE AUTHOR

Mark Lee Webb is a poet, photographer, and musician. He received his MFA in Creative Writing from Queens University of Charlotte. He has published several poetry chapbooks, and his work has appeared in many literary journals. His photography has been selected for several juried exhibitions, such as WideOpen 2020. *The Penn Review* used two of his photographs for the covers of their 2019 issue. Mark is also a jazz drummer, playing regularly with The JMB Band. He makes his home in Louisville, Kentucky with his wife, folk musician Molly McCormack.

www.ingramcontent.com/pod-product-compliance
Lightning Source LLC
LaVergne TN
LVHW040159080526
838202LV00042B/3235